A Pilgrim's Journal

Robert Faricy

Sheed & Ward

For Jane Stier, O.S.U.

Chapter nine of this book is a revision of material previously published in *Medjugorje Up Close*, by L. Rooney and R. Faricy (Franciscan Herald Press, Chicago, 1986).

Sheed & Ward™ is a service of National Catholic Reporter Publishing Company, Inc.

Library of Congress Catalog Card Number: 89-60634

ISBN: 1-55612-259-4

Published by: Sheed & Ward
115 E. Armour Blvd. P.O. Box 419492
Kansas City, MO 64141-6492

To order, call: (800) 333-7373

Contents

A spring of love gushed from my heart,
And I blessed them . . .
The selfsame moment, I could pray;
And from my neck so free
The Albatross fell off, and sank
Like lead into the sea.

—Samuel Taylor Coleridge,
"The Rhyme of the Ancient Mariner," Part IV

1

Places in Faith:
A Note to the Reader

1

Religious experience takes place in concrete settings, has body in the circumstances. It is the principle of the Incarnation of God in Jesus of Nazareth: that matter is the proper vehicle of spirit.

This book describes my own religious experience as it took shape in various places. Giving talks and retreats and attending meetings, I have travelled to several countries. In some of these travels, I have felt my Christian faith strongly affected by my surroundings. I took notes on the spot, and I have organized them into the succeeding chapters of this book.

Some chapters resulted from several trips to the same place: Bucharest, Derry, Lagos, for example. The chapter on Rome developed during my sixteen years of living in its center.

Most places that I have visited and that influenced my faith have not become chapters. Three weeks of giving retreats to priests in Manila just before the fall of Marcos gave me over forty-five pages of notes. But I found myself too close emotionally to the Filipino turmoil to write about it, even to put my impressions on paper. Extended visits to Australia kept me so busy that I found no time to take notes. Visits to India, to Japan, and to Indonesia had an effect on me, stunned me. But the brief experience of cultures so far removed from my own, so exotic in comparison with my ordinary experience, left me unable to sort out my impressions.

But in certain cases I could express what I saw and heard, what helped form my faith, what touched my relationship with the Lord. A new place acts as a new context for faith in God. The new geographical space impinges on my faith and molds my inner space, gives it new aspects, a new dimension. It can lead me closer to the Lord.

New places unsettle me a little. The uprootedness of travelling to a new city shakes me loose from my habitual perspectives. It helps me to see more clearly: to see myself, the world around me, and the Lord present in all places. Through travel I understand better where I'm from, who I am, what I believe and in whom.

2

Every journey is a kind of pilgrimage. Life itself is a journey and a pilgrimage to God. Every Christian life is an eschatological journey from where-I-am-now to my-future-somehow-in-God. My travels from one place to another can shed light on the meaning of the journey of my life and on the meaning of the journey in history of humankind.

The chapters that follow have the structure of a faith journey. I went to the places of the following chapters pretty much in the chronological order of their sequence in the book. The next chapter, about two visits to Bucharest, the capital of Rumania, tells of my experience of God's absence in a communist culture. Some faith journeys, perhaps many, begin with an experience of the absence of God. Following chapters try to show God's presence in suffering: in the divisions in Jerusalem, in the civil war of Northern Ireland, and in the disoriented society of Zimbabwe. Suffering marks every faith journey.

Chapter Seven, on Lagos, Nigeria, is about Christian hope, always the motive force of every journey in faith. The eighth chapter, on Rome, talks about God's presence in a civilization. The following three chapters describe in different ways the peace that God's presence gives.

Navigational aids that science discovers in nature, such as the dance of bees, can help us to know our own nature and how we navigate. The travels described here are a kind of bee's dance. They teach me, and—I hope—you, reading this, something about how we navigate the sea of life on our journey to God.

3

I wrote several of the following chapters as magazine articles that appeared in *The Tablet, Commonweal,* and *America.* I have brought them together, with new material, into a book about places I have been— geographical places but also faith places, places on the planet and places on the interior terrain of personal faith.

I visited these geographical places with an attitude of Christian faith. I saw them, tried to understand them, reflected on my experience and wrote about it, all from a Christian faith perspective. This visiting, seeing, understanding, reflecting, writing, has broadened and deepened my own Christian faith outlook on the world I live in. I hope that reading this book will, in some way and to some degree, do the same for you.

The book is about travels, journeys: trips made by flying, taking trains, driving a car, walking. Too, and especially, this book tells about what and how I have grown in my Christian faith. My exterior journeys in the space on the globe have stimulated interior journeys in faith in the inner space of my heart. So I pray that, as you read about my outer and inner journeys and experiences, the Lord will bless you with a deepening awareness of your own inner journey and with an always fuller experience of faith in him.

2

Bucharest:
The Absence of God
in a Communist City

1

There has been talk in recent years of alternative life styles. Particularly now, in the light of energy crises, food shortages and starvation for many in the world, and the increasingly clear limits of natural resources, we are taking seriously the idea that Europeans and Americans will simply have to change their life style. The directions of change seem evident: towards a world society in which there will be a more equitable distribution of goods, towards a certain egalitarianism and more simplicity of life, perhaps towards stronger governmental authority to assure greater equity, frugality, simplicity. One alternative life style that has taken this general direction is that of Rumania; here are my impressions of a visit to the capital, Bucharest, written in my hotel room in the center of the city.

The outlet for my electric razor has a timer; after exactly forty seconds, the current shuts off. I've learned to shave in precisely forty seconds, which does seem to be the minimum possible time. There is no wastepaper basket in my room; in Rumania, nothing is wasted. Although it is a luxury hotel, and the summer weather is heavy and hot, there is no air conditioning. In the six-bulb chandelier, there is only one bulb.

4

At breakfast in the hotel dining room, there is one of everything for each person, but only one. One pat of butter, one small tin of marmalade, one slice of cheese. There are no seconds and no substitutions. If there is tea (one tea bag for each person), there is no coffee; if coffee, no tea. In other words, there is enough for everyone, but nothing extra or special for anyone. You must like what you get, because you can't always get what you like.

Outside the hotel, in downtown Bucharest, the same principle holds—an egalitarianism in which there is a sufficiency for each, but not much choice and no extras. There are very few movie theaters, but they are packed. A World War II John Wayne movie last night had every seat filled. The films have long runs. There is some theater, both Rumanian and American plays (George Abbott, for instance). There are concerts and an opera. But, for most people, a night on the town is walking up and down the sidewalk of one of the broad main streets, stopping in one of the stand-up beer parlors to wait in a long line for a large beer, and then taking the bus home.

There are *many* buses; public transportation is cheap and excellent. But it is crowded, even at six in the morning, for there are few automobiles. There is no traffic, and so no traffic problem—which is just as well, since the Rumanians do not seem to be very good drivers.

There is a certain drabness or tackiness about Bucharest that goes beyond the sameness and egalitarianism of the popular culture. There is a great lack of style, of flair, of élan. The clothes, in the stores (they are not elegant enough to be shops) and on the people, are dumpy. The bands that play at the Saturday and Sunday night wedding parties in the hotel dining rooms sound like Lawrence Welk playing Dixieland in a polka beat with a three-man combo. The buildings are ugly.

The people seem well enough off (no poor, no rich) and reasonably contented. They are orderly; most well-behaved, docile, occasionally polite but rarely gracious. They do not smile.

2

What holds society together in Rumania is authority. Authority is the bond of Rumanian unity. This authority is centralized in Nicolae Ceausescu, the president, who runs the country single-handedly. One of his counselors told me that the people need a strong central authority; otherwise, they will not make progress.

And the Rumanians are docile. Even as I write this, a caravan of buses, headed by a police car with light flashing and siren blasting, is taking a herd of Bucharestians to line the road to the airport. Standing in the rain, they will dutifully wave at a friendly country's visiting premier and his staff as they are driven to their plane after the state visit to President Ceausescu. Then the buses will take the people back to the center of the city.

It is a tightly-controlled society. You cannot buy a magazine or a newspaper from any non-communist country; I could not find one anywhere in Bucharest. The Bucharest newspaper is one small sheet folded double. What news there is is almost all Rumanian, and all political. I've learned enough Rumanian to read the local paper, but it doesn't tell me anything. After only some days in Bucharest, I feel completely cut off from what is going on in the world.

Vertical (authority) relationships are more important than horizontal relationships. And there is a lack of warmth and spontaneity in casual human encounters. On the street, when a man with an unlit cigarette is looking for a light, he does not ask for one. He finds someone who is already smoking and, wordlessly, lights his cigarette from the other's. No matches or lighter fuel are consumed. And the relationship has been strictly functional, to the point of lacking any verbal communication. Functional, frugal, disinterested. There is a coldness about the people of Bucharest that does not at all correspond to the tourist brochures ("the joyous nature of the Bucharestians").

It is definitely not a "consumer society." The social structure is ordered not to the consumer but to economic progress, to order, and to smooth functioning. This seems particularly true of the tourist industry.

The Rumanian government has made enormous efforts to build up tourism, to attract tourists from other countries, especially from Europe and North America. There is a large and quite bureaucratic tourist ministry in the center of Bucharest. A new luxury hotel has been built. Promotion campaigns have been under way for some time. But the whole Rumanian tourist industry is ordered not to the tourist, not to the consumer, but rather to pleasing central authority by being well-behaved, docile, frugal, efficient, orderly. So, from the tourist-consumer's point of view, it does not work. It is difficult, and sometimes impossible, to make hotel reservations, get a taxi, get a receipt, change your room, get ice, make a phone call. The tourist industry is not trying to please the tourist; it is trying to please the government. It does not seem to realize that it cannot succeed as an industry unless it pleases the tourist.

3

The national church is the Rumanian Orthodox Church, which is supported and controlled by the government. It is a part of the state system, completely subject to governmental authority. In the late 1940s, the Rumanian-rite Roman Catholic Church was suppressed. All the bishops, priests and nuns were put in concentration camps, and all the Rumanian-rite Catholics were declared to be, from then on, members of the Rumanian Orthodox Church. Rumanian-rite Roman Catholicism remains severely outlawed. Officially, of course, full freedom of religion is proclaimed.

Even the state church is quite restricted. I was told at the Orthodox seminary in Bucharest that only one candidate can be accepted for every five or six who apply. I have been unable to buy a New Testament in any language, including Rumanian, anywhere in Bucharest, even at the seminary. A visiting Catholic priest might receive permission from the Latin-rite vicar general (there is no Roman Catholic bishop in Bucharest) to say Mass once in a week, but only in the private chapel at the vicar general's house, never in public.

And yet, I like Bucharest. I would like to come back. There is something homey and familiar about it. I woke up yesterday morning with the thought that Rumania is just like my novitiate. At the beginning of my life in a religious order, during the novitiate years, there was order, frugality, docility, drabness, impersonalness, and much, much authority. Rumania is a big novitiate. But without God.

4

Back in Bucharest for an international conference, one of my first acts is to acquire an intestinal infection. A sign in the hotel lobby tells me there is a full-time doctor on duty; I go to the doctor's office.

"Are you the doctor?" I ask the attractive blonde in the doctor's office. Her look is venomous. She examines me and asks me how I feel. She loftily explains that she does not regularly work in a hotel. There are doctors in the hotels only during the conference. This, she explains, is because with all the foreigners coming to Bucharest for the international conference there is danger of some alien germ entering Rumania and perhaps even causing an epidemic. She and other doctors are in the hotels to intercept any foreign germs that might have come into the country. It is to protect Rumania. I tell her I have been attacked by a Rumanian microbe; she seems unconvinced, and writes a prescription for an antibiotic.

The doctor's name is on a badge on her chest. I tell her she has a wonderful first name, Mariana, the name of Jesus' mother and of his grandmother all in one name. She becomes friendlier, shows me pictures of her children, and asks me if I am married. I say no, that I am a Roman Catholic priest. Her expression begins with incomprehension and moves to wary vigilance as she realizes that I am the carrier of a germ beyond her science and far more dangerous than anything she can stamp out with antibiotics.

There is a girl at the desk in the lobby whose job is to help those who are attending the conference; her name is Ana. We speak in French, and I ask her if she has been to Paris. She looks lost and helpless, and tells me that very few university students can leave the country to study, unless they go to Moscow. I ask Ana to tell me what the typical authentic Rumanian dishes are that I should order in the restaurant. She doesn't know. I press the question, and she finally answers, "Pepsi-Cola." I tell her people all over the world drink Pepsi-Cola; it's not authentically Rumanian at all. She's surprised.

We talk further, and Ana tells me that there is an emptiness at the center of her life. I ask if she believes in God. She doesn't. But she thinks maybe that's it, that if she did believe in God, that might fill the emptiness. "What is God?" she asks me. "Is it fate?" We talk for a while about God.

I go to the small church across the street, an Orthodox church, to sit and pray. The Rumanian Orthodox Church is the official church, an arm of the government, but its activities are severely limited, and very few people attend services. The church is empty and quiet. I try to pray, but God is not there. It's not just another case of the spiritual blahs; I feel God's absence; I miss him.

The maid on my floor stops me as I am going to my hotel room, and speaks to me in Rumanian. I catch just enough to know that she wants to buy something from me, something in my room. We go to the room. I've left my rosary on the table, and she wants to buy it from me. I give it to her, ungenerously because I'm thinking that I'll have to say the rosary on my fingers until I leave Rumania and can get a new one. The maid will not let me pay her for doing my laundry.

At eight o'clock in the morning I go to the Orthodox cathedral in the center of Bucharest to make my meditation, thinking that maybe I won't feel God's absence in a cathedral. I'm just in time for a meeting of all the priests in the city; I take a seat unobtrusively in the back of the church. I see only one priest who looks as if he might be under fifty. A distinguished-looking bearded priest begins to speak. I can understand only enough to know that he is talking about loyalty to the principles of Rumanian communism. It is a harangue, a kind of scolding. Then another priest begins to read what looks like a long official document. No one has prayed. I leave, and go to sit on a bench in the park outside the cathedral to begin my meditation. On the bench next to mine sits a very old priest smoking a cigarette. He looks as if he doesn't want to go to the meeting. After about half an hour, he slowly rises and with resignation walks into the cathedral.

We have the weekend free, and on Saturday I take a train to Brasov, a city in the Carpathian Mountains. The people there are mostly of German and Hungarian origin. I find two Roman Catholic churches. One is closed. I go into the other; it's small and old-fashioned, but an altar-table has been set up facing the people. After a while five young men enter and half-sit, half-kneel, all in the same pew. They are quiet. They don't look as if they're praying. They stay only a minute and leave without genuflecting. They remind me of myself at eighteen. I pray for them.

My last day in Bucharest, as I have every day since I arrived, I say Mass in my hotel room. I sit at the small table and, alone, offer Mass for the people of Rumania. I pray that Jesus Christ come into their hearts, and that his presence be active and vital and more typically and authentically Rumanian than Pepsi-Cola. When the time comes for the last blessing, on impulse I rise from the chair and go to the balcony of my room. Standing high above the city, I call down God's blessing on the people of Bucharest in the name of the Father and the Son and the Holy Spirit, and I tell them to go in peace.

3

Jerusalem: Via Dolorosa

1

Jerusalem, the holy city, is a city of hatred. I ask Janet, a volunteer at the religious hospice where I have a room, how she likes it here; she's been here seven months, taking some Bible courses and helping the sisters. "Well, you know," she says, "you hate it, and you love it; you hate it, but it *is* the *holy land*." What does she not like about Jerusalem? The spiritual heaviness, the tensions, the unhappiness. "It's the tensions between the Israelis and the Arabs"; but she implies that it's much more than that. "It's understandable when you look at the whole history." I tell her I don't understand it yet, but I'm trying to learn.

Sister Rosemary asks me if I've read the writings of a certain Protestant theologian who claims that Islam is diabolical, that Allah is not at all the same as the Christian God. The whole thing is a plot of the devil. I tell her where I disagree: that Allah is the same God we worship, and that there seems to be real holiness in Islam. This seems to correspond with her experience. But, she says, when you hear the Moslem prayers sung from the minarets five times a day, you can really believe that it's all diabolical.

Sure enough, about an hour later amplifiers begin blasting. We're in the Arab quarter, and the loudspeakers blare in even through the closed windows, pre-empting attention and making any thought or intellectual concentration impossible. I begin the rosary, uniting myself with Mary praying to the Father, and with the Moslem chants going up to the same

11

God and Father. I find I enter easily into the prayer. I understand nothing of the Arabic singing, and I'm not thinking about the meaning of the *Hail Mary's* I say. But I'm in union with the Mother of Jesus and with the Moslems in this Arab section of the holy city who lift up their hearts to the one God.

The shouting, grating voices call to prayer, but no one seems to be praying. The sisters tell me that the main purpose of the blaring recorded chanting is political. It says that the Arab population is here, and with no intention of leaving.

I wake up early my first morning in Jerusalem, and walk out on the terrace. At four-thirty, before daybreak and sweetly, as though the most natural thing in the world, the Arabic chant begins to come through the minaret amplifiers. It lasts about twenty minutes, waking up the Arab quarter. Lights go on, and the city begins a new day as the day itself begins to dawn. The Moslem prayers have called down God's light on his city.

"They spit at me," Brother Henry tells me at breakfast, "and they call me names." Brother Henry is preparing to open up a Catholic bookstore and catechetical resources center on the Via Dolorosa, and the Arab shopkeepers—who sell souvenirs to the tourists—view his enterprise as serious and threatening competition. They ask him when his provincial superior is going to transfer him out of Jerusalem. And they spit at him. Clearly, the brother is not used to being hated, and he suffers greatly from the dark pressure of surrounding hostility.

It's hard living here in the old city of Jerusalem, Sister Rosemary tells me. Christians are a minority group, fewer than the Jews or the Arabs; the Catholics are an even smaller minority group.

Now the morning sunlight brightens the city. The buildings here are joined together; walkways join the terraces of adjacent houses, and covered and uncovered passageways fasten the city's building units to one another. The sun on the joined terraces makes the Arab quarter dazzle, and the steady murmur of the quarter's voices makes it hum. Standing on the terrace outside my room, I'm reminded of standing on the deck of a battleship in the ocean sun. Jerusalem's old city is like that, everything crowded together, no traffic or even any real streets, people piled in one on top of the other, closely. Too closely, maybe. Tourists, Moslems, Jews, Christians. I can feel what Janet calls the heaviness. A city oppressed by ancient and ever new resentments.

I began to meet these tensions soon after I accepted the invitation to come to Jerusalem to give some talks. In preparation for my visit to the Holy Land, I looked up the address of the Israeli tourist office in Rome, the city where I live, and walked to the number on Via Veneto. The agency is not on the street. I pass through a wide hallway and up a winding staircase; I arrive on a deserted landing where a door shows me a nameplate that says that this is the Israeli tourist agency. I push a doorbell button. I look up at the television camera peering down on me from the ceiling. A voice, electronically distorted, asks me who I am and what I want. I answer the disembodied voice, speaking into the tiny metal grille from which the voice issued. The voice says to come in. I push open the heavy door. The office is a fortress held by two grim and tough-looking men with "police" written across their faces in the international script that even illiterates can read. The older man deigns to hand me some maps and brochures. Neither of them has the customary salesman-like graciousness of a tourist agent. I take my paper booty and leave the fortress, conscious only of the terrible fear that hides these men in their second-floor bunker. Fear of what? Arab terrorists, bombs, raids? The fear clings to me and dissipates only out on the Via Veneto where hundreds of people walk, unaware of dangers, innocent, vulnerable.

The day of my flight, I go to the El Al desk at the Rome airport to check in. A security guard intercepts me just before I get to the check-in counter, examines the contents of my bag, and asks me many questions about who I am, what I do, why I want to go to Israel, what I will do there, who invited me and why, and what written evidence I have of the invitation. After fifteen minutes, a senior security officer interrogates me, asking the same questions. I give the same answers. The security people try hard, unsuccessfully, not to intimidate me.

I will be less intimidated but more thoroughly searched when I leave Israel. At the Tel Aviv airport, hard-eyed boys and girls will pass me from one to the other for a thirty-minute grilling and examination of each item in my bag and on my body. A man travelling alone with only hand luggage looks dangerous.

2

And now I'm living for a few days just off the Via Dolorosa, where Jesus carried his cross to Calvary. Just down the street, he was flogged nearly to death. They put a circle of thorns on his head just a few yards from where I write this. They mocked him, and they spat on him and called him names.

I find Jesus on the stone pavement, the *lithostratos,* where he was mocked, and crowned with thorns. The sisters at the Ecce Homo convent have unearthed it, and continue their archaeological research into the possibility that Jesus humbled and beaten really stood here. I think he did.

And I find Jesus again, early my second morning in Jerusalem, at the end of the Via Dolorosa in the Church of the Holy Sepulcher. He's here in the church, and especially on Mount Calvary (up a winding staircase to a chapel; I put my hand through a hole and touch the rock where the cross stood) and in the holy sepulcher itself, the empty tomb from which Jesus rose on the first Easter morning. The tiny sepulcher room seems filled with his presence; the tomb is no longer empty, but full of the risen Jesus.

And I find him in the rumpled Franciscan friars, lined up in a row as though for an inspection they'd never pass, chanting the morning liturgical office. And in the little group of Orthodox celebrating Mass in a chapel the size of a small closet attached to and just behind the burial place of Jesus' broken body; they chant "Kyrie eleison," and with them I lift my heart to God to receive his mercy.

A spirit of reverence, of worship, and of humble prayer pervades the Church of the Holy Sepulcher. I wasn't prepared for it; I wasn't ready to find Jesus there. I approached the church with a cynical eye, expecting the same commercial hubbub and absence of God that I experienced along the Via Dolorosa. But Jesus found me and wiped my cynicism away.

In the Church of the Holy Sepulcher, Jesus shows himself in the pilgrims who come to find him there, in the Eucharist, and in the pervading atmosphere of a strongly holy place. Why does Jesus not show himself on the Via Dolorosa? Why can I not find him where he carried his cross? Perhaps my Via Dolorosa experience, the experience of God's absence—in such contrast with my experience of his presence in the Holy Sepulcher Church—is the way it should be.

At the end of his own Via Dolorosa, Jesus cried out to God, "Why have you abandoned me?" The Via Dolorosa, the painful road, is a way of the cross, an experience of God's absence, a suffering journey.

The sisters at Ecce Homo give me a booklet on *Finding Jesus at the Holy Places Today*. A card inside the front cover advises me, "Do not fix your eyes on the affliction surrounding you; turn your eyes upon the risen Lord." Page one of the booklet tells me that I will not normally find Jesus "in the Via Dolorosa where the cries of the shopkeepers fill the air"; "at times it will be difficult . . . to find Jesus at the sites of his sufferings."

But I do find him here in the Via Dolorosa, of course. He's here suffering in Brother Henry, spat on and hated, hurt and defensive; Jesus suffers in him. He's suffering in Sister Rosemary, trying to find a theological reason for her resentment against the Moslems. He suffers in Janet, baffled by the old city's negativity, here to find Jesus and finding a city of hates. He suffers in the Arabs, afraid, clutching their human dignity like final scraps of clothing. And he weeps again over his chosen people.

Stripped, mocked, hated, spat on, Jesus is here. I see him in my brothers and sisters along the Via Dolorosa.

4

The Way
of the Cross in Derry

1

In Northern Ireland, at the Belfast bus station ticket-window, I ask the lady to direct me to the toilet. She smiles warmly and says, "They blew it up." Violence, fallen on hard times, is reduced to the ludicrous. Blowing up the toilet.

"Controlled area," the signs say. "No vehicle many be left unattended." An unattended vehicle could be a car-bomb, an automobile rigged to explode at a given time or on signal. Graffiti in the Catholic ghettos say, "R.U.C. Keep Out" (the R.U.C. is the Royal Ulster Constabulary—the police force) and "VOTE I.R.A."

Violence lies heavily across Northern Ireland like the gun-metal grey skies. Violence is heavy in the hard, cold air. The tension of violence permeates the atmosphere and dominates conversation.

The Mother General whom I visit in Belfast, a sweet holy woman, speaks casually of "the other side" and of "ours." Her sisters teach in Catholic elementary and secondary schools in Belfast, where the younger children look up to the teenagers, and where the teenagers are either I.R.A. soldiers or strong sympathizers. The sisters tell me stories about their pupils, the boy shot dead at sixteen because he belonged to the I.R.A., the two girls arrested and detained for stealing three tooth-

16

picks from a shop, the abuse and humiliation their students undergo from the police and the British Army. No one can see the end of the violence.

Sister Fiona drives me to the city of Derry, where I am to give three talks to members of the Catholic Charismatic Renewal. We shall be stopped, she tells me, by the Royal Ulster Constabulary, the overwhelmingly Protestant police force of Northern Ireland. "Do they stop everyone?" I ask. "No," the sister responds, "but they stop everyone with *BUI* number-plates." *BUI*, she tells me, is the designation for Derry. Unlike most of Northern Ireland, Derry has a strong Catholic majority, so most people on the road with Derry number-plates are Catholic.

A sign says, "Check point ahead; switch off headlights." The police at the roadblock motion the cars ahead of us to pass on through, but they flag us over to the side of the road. The sister gets out, then returns to say that they want to see my identifying documents. I get out and show my American passport to a frightened policeman with ice-cold, fear-stricken eyes and an anxiety-provoked grin. I could, after all, be a terrorist disguised by my Roman collar. Sister Fiona's undisguised hostility towards the policeman is manifest in her unsmiling brusqueness; it is a side of a religious sister that I have never seen before in all my Catholic life.

2

As we approach Derry, the signs invariably read "Londonderry." I ask Sister Fiona what the real name of the city is. "Derry," she replies. "No one calls it Londonderry." Londonderry is the name the English gave it when they took Derry by force in the seventeenth century. Londonderry is the official British name, the name on all the city signs, documents, buildings. No Catholic ever uses it. The city council has voted to call itself the "Derry City Council," but the council's name notwithstanding, the city's name remains Londonderry. Only the British government could change the insulting name, and of course they never will.

Derry is divided by the River Foyle, running into the North Sea. East of the Foyle are the Protestants. The Catholics live west of the river. The Catholic section in the heart of Derry is called the "Bogside." Sometimes the name "Bogside" is applied to the total Catholic area; "Bogside" means "Catholic." About sixty percent of the Catholic men here have no work. The city is clean, however, and I see no really poor people, no slums. The houses are neat, kept up, painted. British social benefits have kept the Catholics from destitution while keeping them jobless and humbled. There is no factory in Derry, no real industry of any kind in the Derry area. Only the industry of oppression, of terror, of producing fear.

The opening Mass for the "Derry Diocesan Charismatic Renewal Conference" takes place on Friday evening in Saint Columba's Church, known as the "Long Tower," the oldest church in the city, built on the site of Columba's first monastery. Saint Columba is the patron saint of Derry. The name "Derry" comes from the Gaelic "Doire," meaning "oak grove." The ancient name of the city was "Doire, Colmcille"— "Columba's Oak Grove." Saint Columba's, the Long Tower Church, lies at the heart of the Bogside, a center of hope and comfort for the wounded Catholic community.

My room for the night is in a parish rectory. The next morning, eating breakfast in the kitchen, I tell the housekeeper how well I slept, remarking, "It's quiet here." "Now, yes," she says, "but not always." When some of the men in prison went on hunger strike, even to death, the nights were not so quiet. People would bang on rubbish-bins and make a clamorous noise during the night. "Why?" I ask the housekeeper. "Rejoicing," she says, "rejoicing somebody died, rejoicing in the victory." The death of a Catholic prisoner who starved himself to death is seen as a victory, a resurrection, a triumph over the English.

After breakfast, on the way to the conference where I will give my talks, the priest driver says, to me and to the two priests in the back seat, "They shot three this morning." Then there is silence in the car. I break it with a question: "Who got shot?" "Three of the boys," the driver answers. I ask, "Did they have guns, or what?" "Maybe," he said; "maybe one had a gun." A British Army foot patrol shot them. The Northern Ireland security forces no longer take prisoners. According to their policy now, "They shoot to kill," says the priest driving the car. We go on in silence. I learn later that the three young men, ages sixteen, nineteen and twenty, tried to surrender. Witnesses heard them plead with the police, "For the love of God, don't shoot, don't shoot!"

A large black and white painted sign reads, "YOU ARE NOW ENTERING FREE DERRY." There is a big splotch where someone has thrown a tin of yellow paint at the sign; it goes well with the black and white.

Derry city-center on Saturday morning: heavy grey clouds that come down almost to the heads of the crowds of people walking around, almost no traffic. The people, like the clouds, are drab, colorless grey, moving but seeming to stand still.

In the evening after supper, about seven o'clock, I take a walk through the center of the city. The deserted streets and the closed shops tell me that the Derry people stay in at night, even on Saturday night. I see only a few people; they are walking to the evening session of the conference. Suddenly an armed motor vehicle turns into Ferryquay Avenue, where I am walking, and moves slowly down the middle of the road. As it passes me, I can look into the open back; the vehicle is filled with British soldiers in full combat dress, rifles held at the ready vertically between their knees. They do not talk. They look young, about eighteen or twenty years old. On top of the motor vehicle sits another young soldier with a machine gun; the gun is horizontal, trained on a possible target ahead, a little to the right or a little to the left. A second armed vehicle, with another boy-soldier and machine gun on top, comes after the first. And then a third.

Impressed and chilled by the procession under the dark Derry sky, I stop to take notes for the present article. A sister, walking with a few other nuns on their way to the conference, breaks away from her group, crosses the street to me, and says, "Oh, Father, don't be writing like that; they'll arrest you."

They do not arrest me, however. I see no foot patrol, although soldiers do patrol the Catholic section of Derry, and especially the Bogside. They stop young men and frisk them, looking for weapons or any other condemning evidence. They annoy them and they insult them.

At the evening conference I tell the sister I met on my walk how I feel about walking in a town where armed soldiers drive slowly through the main streets. She is fascinated that I have any impression at all; she is used to the army occupation, takes it for granted. Army and police surveillance and harassment are normal, the order of the day. For special occasions, the sister tells me, they fly two or three helicopters for surveillance and harassment. At funeral processions, for instance, the helicopters move in low, noisy and creating strong winds, intimidating those in the religious procession.

3

On Sunday morning, driving again to the conference for my last talk, the priest driver tells me that last night at 10 o'clock the I.R.A. took a Long Tower Church parishioner, Kevin Coyle, out into the back garden of his house and put a bullet through his head. He had been an informer for the British Army and the R.U.C. Most Catholics, the priest assures me, would accept the execution as just punishment.

I have not been able to think of what to say for my last talk. I have no ideas, and I am supposed to speak for at least forty-five minutes. I feel the terror that only the unprepared speaker knows. Even more on this Sunday morning, I feel the terror that settles like thick fog on Derry.

Arriving early at the conference, I meet the man who will drive me to Belfast Airport after my talk, to catch the plane to London, and I tell him how I feel about his town. "Yes," he says, "they come to pick someone up and take him to the police station between midnight and five in the morning." If you hear a car start or a car-door slam in the middle of the night, he says, you get very nervous. They come into his neighborhood about once a week, usually three or four Landrovers filled with armed men. They have come to his house. "They knock loudly to wake you up," he says; "then they give you only a few seconds to answer the door, and then they smash your door down and come into your living room with their guns; they just break in."

The police can hold you for seventy-two hours for questioning, with no charges at all. If they do not find out what they want, my driver says, they let you go after seventy-two hours. Then they pick you up again just outside the station door for another seventy-two hours.

"There are times I think, should we go back to England? We lived there for ten years. They pick up your children here without telling you," the man says. In the last five weeks, the British Army and the R.U.C. have shot seven boys who had stolen cars for a lark. "Joy riders—they know they're not I.R.A. (the I.R.A. drive carefully)—they just shoot them."

The Sunday morning session begins with prayers and hymns. I go up on the stage and sit down; I still do not know what I will say for my talk, but for some time now I have had the thought that Derry is walking the way of the cross.

When the moment comes, I go to the speaker's podium. I begin with the First Station: "Jesus is condemned to death." I talk about how all unjust condemnation partakes of the unjust condemnation of Jesus, and how everyone condemned unjustly participates in Jesus' own condemnation. Jesus is humiliated, stripped of dignity, terrorized, unjustly condemned. So is Derry's Catholic population. Seven hundred people listen to me; no one coughs, and no feet are shuffled.

I talk and pray my way through the fourteen Stations of the Cross, applying them to Derry with no difficulty. At the fourteenth station, "Jesus is placed in the tomb," I say that Mary, the mother of Jesus, bends over the broken city of Derry now just as she then bent over the broken body of her son Jesus. She grieved over Jesus, and she grieves over Derry. We all say a "Hail Mary" together.

5

London Ritz

1

Maybe the phrase "putting on the ritz," meaning to act very rich, glitzy rich, high class, upper crust with money, comes from London's Ritz Hotel. Certainly, it is ritzy, rich, high class. The fire escape has an expensive carpet, live—not artificial—plants, and good framed prints on the walls. And that's just the fire escape. The Ritz stationery is heavy weight paper, with the name of the hotel on it. The men's room has absolutely everything you would ever need, and much you would never expect to find in a men's room. That includes clothes brushes—several, I suppose in case several men want to brush their suits all at the same time. Hand towels, combs, hair brushes, and much more. And an attendant, quite high class and ritzy, who makes me feel not inferior but high class and ritzy myself.

The other chapters in this book tell about cities or at least small towns. This chapter is no exception except that the Ritz is more than a town or a city or another country. The Ritz stands across the street from the Green Park underground station in London, on the edge of Piccadilly, looking down somewhat contemptuously on the other side of the street where the fashionable district of Mayfair begins, as another world. Like Mars or Pluto. Another planet.

2

Do not think that I have ever stayed at the Ritz. I could never afford the prices. I cannot afford even to have tea at the Ritz. But I go there.

I am here now at the Ritz with my sister. A nun, she has temporarily taken off her veil and put it in her purse. "I would not want anyone to see a *nun* in the *Ritz*," she says. Apparently, this would disedify the Ritz's clientele. She still looks exactly like a nun. My sister has never before visited the Ritz Hotel. She looks around her in awe. So do I. Great stuff.

Why do I come to the London Ritz? To sit comfortably in the spacious Louis XVI decor, ritzy lobby. To sit at one of the writing desks and write various things, like this, on the fabulous Ritz stationery. To use the men's room. To wander around. I enjoy the Ritz.

And coming to the Ritz reminds me, always, of who I am and of what I am doing in this world. I am poor, and I will stay that way by choice. I am not working for an earthly crown. My heart is in heaven, because that is where my treasure is. I am, I want to be, poor with Jesus poor, crucified to the world and the world to me. If I boast, I boast in the Lord. If I glory, I glory in my poverty and in my infirmities because Jesus' strength is made perfect in my weakness.

I go to the Ritz partly because I enjoy it and partly because it stands for the opposite of what I am and what I want to do in this world. Every short visit to that other world of the Ritz tells me that I have here no lasting city. My city is the New Jerusalem that will come down from heaven, Jesus' bride, my mother.

My sister and I walk out the front door, past the three elegantly uniformed doormen, and cross the street. We turn and look at the hotel. We say good-bye to the Ritz.

6

Zimbabwe
After the Apocalypse

The Republic of South Africa has begun its apocalypse and moves disastrously toward an ending and some kind of a new beginning. In Zimbabwe, the world has already ended. Zimbabwe has had its apocalypse in the revolution against Ian Smith's Rhodesian government. Independence in 1981 ended the old world. It resulted not in a new heaven and a new earth but, rather, in a Marxist purgatory.

1

The people seated at table with me this evening are all white, longtime residents here in Harare, formerly Salisbury, the nation's capital. They do not know the world ended in 1981, and they act just as they did before. Like the characters in C.S. Lewis' novel *The Great Divorce*, they maintain their dignity and the elegant manner that comes from good breeding, unaware that they now reside in purgatory. The black man standing immaculately at the end of the table in his servant's jacket gives them no clues. Impassive, he pretends he cannot hear the conversation, which turns to the Catholic Church in Zimbabwe. The missionary orders have stopped sending new men—unfairly, all at table agree, except perhaps the black servant who remains like a statue. No one laments the lack of African vocations.

24

The priests with me at dinner, quite elderly, came decades ago. They claim to understand the Africans, and maybe they really do; however, they appear almost totally out of contact with the surrounding realities. Perhaps because they are a little hard of hearing, they missed the explosion in 1981, when the world ended.

The Church gives the impression of a black organization run by white people. Some dioceses have black bishops. But the black archbishop of Harare, for example, leans heavily on his astute and loyal English Jesuit secretary, who guides and protects him like an urbane guardian angel. The Catholics of Harare, white and black, regard the archbishop as weak, afraid, and not important.

My black priest friend tells me, speaking of my white priest dinner companions the evening before, "They are racists; we tell them at meetings that they must treat us differently; but they never change." He adds, his voice rising, "That is why there are no vocations!"

An elderly white priest laughingly refers to the Catholic Center at the Harare Cathedral as "the cheapest brothel in town." I ask what activities take place there. "Snooker tournaments and the like—lots of drinking." The bar at the center, unlike other bars, remains open on Sundays. The patrons are white. "Frightfully expensive, too expensive for the blacks," the priest tells me.

The largest Catholic charismatic prayer group, almost entirely African, met at the center every Sunday afternoon until recently. The white woman appointed by the archbishop to run the center made them enter by the rear door. The bar patrons complained about the noisy singing, and the charismatics were told they could no longer meet at the center. The group, unable to find a place to meet, has temporarily disbanded. "That woman," the elderly priest tells me, "wants to become a millionaire as quickly as possible—or so they say."

White society and black society seem to run on parallel and independent tracks. The only exchanges appear to be commercial—buying and selling from one another, or master-servant relationships where black serves white. Life styles differ, and social contact is infrequent.

2

Traditional religion in Zimbabwe holds that ancestral spirits return to inhabit the bodies and souls of their living descendants. Witchcraft is rampant. And curses and spells are the stuff of everyday life.

Commonly, African Zimbabweans invite the souls of their deceased ancestors to enter their bodies. This practice forms the central core of traditional religions in Zimbabwe. As a result, spirit possession holds a high place in traditional religion and culture, with the usual resulting trance states, spirit-induced ecstasies, and emphasis on magic of all kinds.

An African priest in Bulawayo assures me that possession by ancestral spirits forms an important part of Catholicism's inculturation here in Zimbabwe. He sees no difficulty in simply assimilating the ancestral spirit doctrines and practices into Catholicism.

Startled by such views from a priest, I ask a European missionary what they teach about ancestral spirits in the national seminary. He tells me that the professors stand divided on the issue, and that, reportedly, at least one African bishop in Zimbabwe strongly holds the traditional African ideas on ancestral spirits. When I point out that the traditional African ideas and practices go directly contrary to Catholic teaching and surely cause serious problems, he shrugs.

The only strong opposition to ancestral spirit possession among Catholics that I could find belongs to the Catholic charismatic renewal, a fledgling and struggling movement with few members. The Catholic charismatics that I spoke to told me that spirit possession among Catholics is not at all uncommon, and that many, especially men, have to formally renounce such beliefs and practices and be freed from them through prayer before they are capable of using the common charismatic gifts of the Spirit such as praying in tongues.

In the charismatic renewal, the differences between white and black Zimbabweans can be seen clearly. The white population in Zimbabwe numbers only about two hundred thousand, or a little over two percent of the total population. And the white people continue to leave at a rate of about six thousand a year. Nevertheless, there are some predominantly white charismatic prayer groups in Harare. Mostly middle-aged whites, they pray decorously.

The black and colored prayer groups, composed largely of young people, are expanding rapidly—Zimbabwe is a youthful country with over half its population under fifteen years of age. And they pray exuberantly, sing loudly, praise God with no inhibitions and with echoes of traditional culture. An elderly white woman, with me at a black prayer meeting, muttered to me disdainfully, "Pure hysteria." It is not hysteria, however, but uninhibited Catholic pentecostalism with a strong African cast.

Zimbabwe Africans, with their tradition of possession by ancestral spirits, take naturally to pentecostalism's Spirit-filled manifestations. Pentecostal sects proliferate—over one thousand in Zimbabwe. The future of the Catholic charismatic renewal looks promising in Zimbabwe, although its African exuberance should increasingly disconcert the staid missionaries, mostly British and German.

3

The Catholic Church in Zimbabwe stays outside politics with very few exceptions. Furthermore, religion seems to be an ineffectual formalism with no practical import. The Prime Minister, Robert Mugabe, and most of his cabinet are Catholics. No one seems to know whether any of them practice their faith. The consensus is: probably not.

Parliamentary sessions always begin with prayers, but they appear to be a mere formality. Religion was taught in all government primary and secondary schools until not long ago. It was simply dropped from the curriculum. To my knowledge, no one and no church protested.

In fact, the government professes to be Marxist. The nation's best friends and supporters are North Korea, China, Rumania, and Bulgaria. Zimbabwe's Marxism, however, appears unsophisticated and superficial. The official documents and the newspapers give every citizen the title of "comrade." Government speakers pay lip service to Marx's name, but they rarely if ever mention any of his ideas.

The economy, in fact, is capitalist. Zimbabwe depends heavily on the South African economy. As the South African economy crumbles and the rand weakens, Zimbabwe's economy will suffer. Further, about ninety percent of all overseas imports to and exports from Zimbabwe pass to the sea by South African rail. The other ten percent goes to the quite inadequate port of Beira in Mozambique by a rail line protected from Mozambican guerillas and bandits, with only partial success, by a large contingent of Zimbabwe's army. If war breaks out in South Africa and the railway becomes inoperable, Zimbabwe will be almost completely cut off from its overseas trade.

"Socialism" in Zimbabwe means "communism." But the country's communism is less economic than political. Mugabe appears to follow the political model of Rumania. He and his party, ZANU (Zimbabwe African National Union), have decided to make the nation a one-party state. And they work hard at the process of eliminating the other parties.

The two parties made up mostly of whites have a diminishing influence. ZANU knows that, within a year or so, they will have negligible importance. The other African party, ZAPU (Zimbabwe African People's Union), led by Joshua Nkomo, is a real problem. The professed plan of ZANU is to simply eliminate ZAPU.

One of ZANU's representatives in parliament has proposed seriously, with the sometimes amusing ingenuousness that characterizes Zimbabwe political statements, that the two parties merge: ZAPU could drop the last two letters of its name, and ZANU could drop the first two letters. The resulting party, then, would be called ZANU.

Another ZANU member of parliament recently suggested that Zimbabwe declare war on ZAPU and "wipe out this ZAPU and arrest its top leadership . . . ZAPU must be banned and its leadership locked up" (Mr. Tongogara, *Parliamentary Debates,* vol. 12, no. 15, 20 August 1985, col. 686-687).

The police have already raided Nkomo's house and at present are investigating the documents they seized. ZANU politicians regularly, in parliament and in the newspapers, cry out for his imprisonment. What keeps Nkomo out of prison is his restraining influence on ZAPU militants. Mugabe knows that with Nkomo removed, the armed bands of ZAPU dissidents that roam southern Zimbabwe would be even more of a problem than they now are.

Will Joshua Nkomo and his ZAPU eventually go the way of Ndabaningi Sithole (out of the country—the government will not renew his passport), Bishop Muzorewa (who fled the country after his defeat in the last election) and their followers? It seems most unlikely. ZAPU has a powerful tribal base.

Of the eight and a half million people in Zimbabwe, about seven million belong to Shona-speaking tribes. The Matabele number over a million, a strong minority. The Shona party is ZANU. Most of the Matabele support ZAPU. The Matabele people live in the south; their unofficial capital is Bulawayo.

In 1963, after agitation in the black reserves of Rhodesia, the African National Congress Party split into two factions, ZANU (Sithole, succeeded by Mugabe) and ZAPU (Nkomo). That same year, both parties were banned and their leaderships interned.

The Shona-speakers back Mugabe. The Matabele back Nkomo. Even though Mugabe calls for a one-party state and publicly invites Nkomo and ZAPU to join ZANU, he knows that only forceful repression will weaken and eventually destroy the opposition party. He is confronted not only with minority party, but with a hostile and warlike tribe who speak their own language, have their own customs, and possess the fierce spirit of their cousins, the South African Zulus.

Consequently, Mugabe has for some time now carried on a reign of terror in Matabeleland. People active in ZAPU regularly disappear. Matabeleland looks like an occupied country. In effect, ridiculous as it sounds, Zimbabwe *has* declared war on ZAPU.

4

Coming in to Bulawayo from the airport, we meet a roadblock manned by government police. My driver explains that they do this to check documents and "to be sure the vehicles are up to specifications." But the police neither ask for our documents nor examine the car. The roadblock has intimidation as its purpose, and I do feel intimidated. I feel outright fear later, when I walk past the "Stops and Ross Camp" just behind the Catholic bishop's house and the Dominican sisters' convent. This is the principal police base in Matabeleland. As in all the police camps in the south, the C.I.O. (Central Intelligence Organization, modeled on the K.G.B.) does its torturing and killing here.

The main days for torturing seem to be Monday, Tuesday, and Wednesday. At least, local residents tell me, that is when you can hear the screaming—especially at night. They tell me that the C.I.O. tortures, sometimes to death, in an eight-cell block in the center of the quite extensive camp. But they still hear screams hundreds of yards away. The C.I.O. uses modern methods of torture, including electric shock. They operate directly under Prime Minister Mugabe, and answer only to him. The Bulawayo newspaper for August 28, 1985 quotes the Minister of State Security, Comrade Emmerson Munangagwa, "In this region (Matabeleland), security forces, acting in concert with each other, particularly on intelligence pertaining to these dissidents, will be more efficient in their efforts to eradicate these worrisome individuals" (*The Chronicle*, p. 1).

What stand has the Catholic Church in Zimbabwe taken with regard to the professed Marxism of the ruling party, ZANU, and the drive toward a one-party state?

In an Easter, 1983, statement the Catholic bishops directly addressed the problem of the brutal suppression of ZAPU and the persecution by the government of the Matabele people. Supporting the government in its efforts to preserve order in Matabeleland, the bishops condemn "methods which have been adopted . . . and have degenerated into brutality and atrocity," bringing about "the maiming and death of hundreds and hundreds of innocent people." The bishops state that "the facts point to a reign of terror caused by wanton killings, woundings, beatings, burnings and rapings." They point to starvation in some areas due to government troops' having deliberately cut off supplies of food and any access to food. And they "appeal to the government to use its authority to put an immediate stop to these excesses" (*Reconciliation Is Still Possible*, Easter, 1983).

In a later pastoral statement of January 1, 1985, the bishops again say that they "are deeply saddened by the suffering of many people and the senseless loss of life caused by disunity, hatred and ruthless hunger for power." This recent statement is weaker than the 1983 pastoral letter. But both statements are courageous.

Having a cup of tea with a lay official of the Catholic Justice and Peace Commission, I ask why the commission has made no statement concerning the brutalities and atrocities of government police and soldiers in Matabeleland. He looks frightened, and well he might be. No statement is planned.

The bishops have also confronted the Marxist orientation of the government. In their pastoral statement of January 1, 1984 they state their clear opposition to certain Marxist principles: atheism, class warfare as a means of positive transformation of society, and government force when persuasion fails.

But in Zimbabwe, government authorities do not listen to the voice of religion. Somehow, the Catholic Church has made itself irrelevant in the area of national moral problems.

7

Lagos:
The End of the World

1

It's been eight years since my last trip to Nigeria, and I'm surprised to find the boarding lounge in the Rome airport packed and overflowing with passengers. On previous trips from Rome to Lagos I travelled on half-filled planes, and most of the passengers were white. Now, ninety percent of the passengers waiting to board Alitalia flight 842 are black. I ask the Alitalia man at the boarding desk why the flight is so crowded. "It's always like this," he says. "They fly up and they buy things and they fly back." "What about the economic reforms?" I ask him. "Haven't they cut down on this kind of travel and buying?" "No," he answers, "if anything, it's worse." Nigeria, I'm beginning to realize, has changed since my last visit. People have money and they spend it.

Why do so many Nigerians make trips to Rome? Some are traders. They take empty suitcases to Italy, stock up on luxury goods, and fly home with full suitcases and with bulging plastic bags. They sell their booty in Nigeria and make enough money to more than pay for the trip. Other Nigerians are on business, or perhaps just tourists; for Nigeria now has money, oil money, and Nigerians can visit other countries.

In the Lagos airport, I pass quickly through an efficient customs procedure. But efficiency ends there. Lagos does not know how to cope with itself. A boom town of over seven million people, it gangles and

32

stumbles awkwardly, glutted with money and growing too fast, suffering through an awful adolescence.

For starters, the Lagos traffic problem has never found a solution. A few years ago, the city government ordered that only cars having an odd first number on their licence plates could travel on Mondays, Wednesdays and Fridays. And only cars having an even number on Tuesdays, Thursdays and Saturdays. For a few weeks it worked. Soon, all those who needed or wanted to drive daily had two cars, one for "odd" days and one for "even" days, and the Lagos traffic went back to normal.

There has been no new telephone book for years, and the old books are completely outdated. The city bus system hardly functions; public transportation has largely given way to private enterprise. Yellow taxis and small yellow minibuses comprise much of the Lagos traffic. Efforts to hold down the rising rate of violent crime consist mainly of frequent roadblocks where soldiers spot-check cars for armed robbers.

The city, too big, too sprawling, expanding too fast, apparently does not know how to govern itself effectively. One cannot, however, compare Lagos to other boom cities like Houston, Texas, or Aberdeen, Scotland. For one thing, Houston and Aberdeen boom precisely as towns. Lago's growth and problems reflect and share in those of the nation. Lagos stands out only as Nigeria's largest urban population. Another difference: Lagos looks, at least to my midwestern American eyes, like a big slum. Side streets full of huge potholes and usually unpaved, no sidewalks, buildings with broken windows, much evident dirt and poverty. Lagos stands for old-fashioned capitalism. A minority grows more wealthy; the poor stay poor. Yet, some wealth does trickle down; and living in a corrugated-roof tumble-down building in Lagos beats living in a mud hut in the bush.

A taxi takes me from the airport to Saint John's parish house, where the Irish missionary pastor explains that he did not meet me at the airport because he thought I was not coming. He never received the telegram I sent two weeks earlier; he shrugs off the missing telegram and the consequent complications as typical everyday happenings in Lagos. "You get used to it," he tells me. "We live in confusion." He seems to enjoy it.

The pastor responds to my telling him that I would have telephoned him from the airport if I had had his telephone number by laughing and saying that, although he has had a telephone for two years, the city has not yet got around to connecting it.

"So much graft," he tells me. You need to bribe a man from the telephone company in order to have a number assigned to you. "I did," he says, "but others gave bigger bribes, and I'm still waiting for a number; there's a lot of corruption in government."

Later, other people tell me of the corruption in the police force, in the government offices, in business. The telephone operator needs a little "dash" (from the Portuguese word for "give") before she can get through on your call. The police at the roadblock need something to warm them up on a cold night. A small sum to the government official in the office to obtain drivers' licenses will get you a form to fill out: "There's a shortage of these forms." A larger sum will get you a form for a passport.

Bribes and payoffs are commonplace, so much so that most European businessmen pay them unquestioningly when doing business here. They understand bribes, graft and corruption as just a part of Nigeria's culture.

Sitting here in my room in the parish house, I can look out of my windows and see construction work going on. The buildings here are new, brightly painted, although apparently poorly built. I can see at least two unfinished buildings—small apartment buildings, as is most of the new housing in Lagos. The contractors do not wait for the city to make streets and to put in sewage; they might have to wait forever. So buildings mushroom without streets, without sewage, sometimes dependent on their own generators for electricity.

Every day, power failures take place; large areas of the city remain without electricity. There is no garbage collection in most areas; the city is filthy. Stripped hulks of automobiles rust along the sides of the main roads, reminders of the dangers of driving in Lagos; no one removes them.

In this neighborhood, children roam everywhere, and everyone seems young. I took a walk after lunch, and saw perhaps two hundred people, none over forty years old. Nigeria has a low average age to go with its high birth-rate. People want children, the more the better. A sister who works in the parish asks me if I will bless some childless couples and pray with them that they have children. Childlessness holds first place in the parish among causes of broken marriages. From the number of children I have seen, I doubt there are many families childless.

Lago's boom in every direction—increasing population, growing urbanization, much building, and business expansion—creates growing-pains and confusion. Large amounts of money around keep prices up, and also tempt people to corruption, especially to graft and bribery. All this puts terrific pressure on everyone. Life's frustrations add up, multiply, and become almost too much to bear. A Nigerian businessman, who suffers from acute high blood pressure, tells me that he has twice flown to London for medical treatment. By the time he saw the doctor, the comparatively slow pace of London life had lowered his blood pressure to normal, and the doctor told him his health was fine. After a week back in Lagos, his blood pressure rose again to its pre-London level.

2

Lagos is a high-pressure city because it is moving rapidly into the future. Future-orientation is, of course, a marked aspect of all contemporary western culture. Nowhere more so than in Lagos. The insurance industry thrives, because who knows what the future holds—and we are going there fast. Credit buying is prevalent. The future, heavily mortgaged, nevertheless holds promise; we can pay then. Education holds first place in the ambitions of almost everyone under thirty—that is, of a large majority of the population. Education now is a heavy investment in the future, an assurance of hope for a future that is already tangible, just ahead, a short way down the road.

This future-orientation makes Lagos a city of hope. Anything seems possible. Imagination, hard work, and a little luck, can build a prosperous and happy life. To be expected in an atmosphere where the impending future holds hope but remains uncertain, Lagos is religious.

The chaotic growth, the immorality, the strong impetus toward the future, the stress on hope, all this gives Lagos an apocalyptic quality. And sure enough, apocalyptic-style religion not only predominates but positively covers Lagos life. In the yellow buses, Pentecostal preachers hold forth, talking sin and redemption from the front of the bus at the glassy-eyed passengers. Pentecostal sects proliferate. A short walk around the block shows the church and active mission center of "Christ Army," the newly-built "Church of the Cherubim and the Seraphim," and two women in white caps and long white dresses—the uniform of the "Aladura" Church.

There are, moreover, hundreds of small mosques just in this neighborhood alone, most of them small private family mosques. From many of them, the Moslem prayers are called out several times daily over loudspeakers.

Religion permeates Lagos life, and everyone has some religion. They talk religion freely. On my walk around the block, a young man, walking a little way in my direction, joins me and asks to what church do I belong. He belongs to the Christ Army Church.

Except for the Moslems, who number not many more than the number of little mosques, the churches here in Lagos are Christian and colorful. Most have a strong Pentecostal flavor.

Even in the Catholic Church, almost every one of the over twenty parishes has an alive and expanding charismatic prayer group. Often, the regular Sunday Mass has a kind of "charismatic" flavor, with much singing, body-swaying, drums, and dynamic preaching.

In Lagos, then, hope in the future finds its roots in religion, and for the most part in Christian religion. I find the same future-orientation in, for example, Houston and Sydney. But hope, in Houston or in Sydney, carries with it an anxious and even panicky worry that I do not find in Lagos. Much hope in the future, here in Lagos, is—ultimately and profoundly—hope in God, hope in Jesus Christ. The Jesus of Lagos Christianity is the risen Lord, the Lord of the future. He holds the future of Lagos, and of each one of us, securely in his hands. We hope in him.

Apocalyptic religion in an apocalyptic city. Maybe the world will finally end with neither a bang nor a whimper but with a slow strangulation brought about by too much money, too many people, too much moral corruption, and a general breakdown of the systems that hold society together. And then the Lord will come a second time, to gather together all who hope in him.

At a Catholic charismatic prayer meeting, a young man prays, almost shouting, eyes shut, hands raised. His voice rises and breaks, his eyes open wide and focus on a distant point, and he cries out, "I see Jesus coming in glory on the clouds of heaven." Automatically, I look to where his eyes are focused; in Lagos, it would not completely surprise me.

8

Rome: Italian Civilization

When I first arrived in Italy I thought it uncivilized. A year later I concluded that it was the last civilized country in the western world. Today, I know that it is the first and perhaps the only truly civilized country I have ever been in.

1

The typical Italian will not hurt anyone. The old jokes—the thinnest book ever written (*Great Italian War Heroes*), and "Who put the four bullets into Mussolini?" ("Fifty Italian sharpshooters")—have a grain of truth. Not because Italians lack courage; far from it. Like everyone else, they do not want to be killed; but, unlike most other peoples, they do not want to kill or even hurt anyone for any reason. They understand not only the evil of war but its hopeless stupidity. Their human decency, their high level of civilization, will not allow them to be expert in barbarities like modern war, bloody riots, and mugging.

The contrast between Italian civilization and American violence is not immediately perceived; it has grown on me, an American, month by month, during the years I have lived in Rome, until it has become striking and obvious. The contrast between a violent culture and a civilization is best seen in attitudes toward violence in the mass media. For example, I have never (not even once) seen real violence depicted on Italian television. Italian newspapers regularly show great outrage and ferocious indignation at any public violence; when the kidnapped young Paul Getty's ear was mailed to his mother, all Italy was sincerely shocked in a way that one cannot imagine Americans reacting.

Italian terrorism, perpetuated by the Red Brigades and similar organizations, strongly repels the average Italian—partly because it is violent, but especially because it puts violence at the service of politics. Nothing is more Italian than politics; and nothing is less Italian than terrorism. Italian terrorism is famous not because it is so much worse than terrorism in, say, France or Germany (it is not), but because the Italians have made it famous by their public shock, revulsion and horror at terrorism. Americans find terrorism menacing. Italians find it absolutely repellent.

Yet, it seems to me that when, as now, Italian society is particularly ill, terrorism becomes almost inevitable. What Italians most disavow surfaces as a symptom of sickness. That which is opposed diametrically to the best and most dominant Italian values comes to the surface as a virulent symptom of the present sickness of Italian society. Terrorism is Italian civilization inside out, Italian civilization at its most antithetical, at its sickest.

Attitudes toward the mafia are quite different here in Italy than in America. Americans consider the mafia part of their contemporary folklore; sure, the mafiosos are outside the law in many cases, ruthless, greedy, unscrupulous. But they are colorful, understandable, interesting, and they have a lot in common with the ordinary American. This is the difference. They have nothing in common with the ordinary Italian. Italians are deeply ashamed of the American mafia, and have no illusions about the mafia in Italy. For an Italian, the mafia is not folkloric; it is criminal, uncivilized, outside human society. Above all, Italians are appalled by mafia violence, repelled by perhaps the very trait that makes the mafia attractive to Americans.

Violence certainly exists in Italy, and it always has. But, unlike the situation in the United States and in some parts of Latin America, violence is in no way a cultural value. Italians do not glorify violence. They find it repugnant; they reject it totally and are horrified by it.

Violence is as American as apple-pie. No Italian would ever say that violence is as Italian as spaghetti.

One spring Sunday afternoon, sitting on a bench in a tiny park off Rome's Piazza Venezia, a friend and I found ourselves between a neo-fascist parade in front of us and a crowd gathering at the communist headquarters behind us. Suddenly the fascists broke ranks and swarmed past us toward the communists; both sides had sticks and clubs, and there was shouting and name-calling. Violence was in the air. The communists drove the fascists back past my friend and me where we remained, stupefied, on our park bench, in the middle of a seething, communist-fascist riot in the center of Rome. We were, of course, uninjured. No one was hurt. Not even a scratch. I did not see a single blow struck. The violence in the air remained in the air; the fascists and the communists would not hurt anyone, not even each other; in Italy, even fascists and communists are civilized.

2

Are Italians, then, more moral than other people? Probably not. But their immorality takes more civilized forms. It is no secret that the Italian government is corrupt, and that bribes are common. There is cheating and stealing in Italy, but what is more common and more evident to the visitor is overcharging. Foreigners are frequently charged too much by taxi drivers, sometimes restaurant bills are padded, and one can be overcharged for even the smallest items—a cigar, a pack of cigarettes, a newspaper. There seem to be a lot of pickpockets, especially on the buses. The point, however, is that the common forms of crime in Italy are non-violent.

Here in Italy one finds little of what has been called "the Protestant ethic." Many of the ethical values that members of mainly Protestant nations think important are just not important to Italians. Punctuality, faithfulness to duty, frankness, exactness—these are not typically Italian virtues. They do not rank as highly as kindness, compassion, helpfulness, gentleness. The Italian ethic is, moreover, the ethic of a country that has been Catholic for many centuries; it is an ethic of compromise, and one that relies heavily on God's mercy without thinking overmuch about his justice. It is an ethic strongly influenced by the sacrament of penance.

American tourists making a European tour are often struck by the contrast between the politeness and helpfulness with which they are greeted by the Italians and the way they are treated by people of other countries to the north of Italy. Italians are kind to each other, and to foreigners; it is part of their civilization. They care, and they want everyone to be happy, to feel good. They will, gladly and at length, give you directions to where you want to go, although the directions may not be accurate. They may nearly run you down with the small cars that they drive wildly—for driving is not so much a means of transportation in Italy as a sport—but they will be sorry, apologetic, smiling humbly at having caused any disturbance or unhappiness.

The average Italian has only a fifth-grade education, but he has a lot of culture. He appreciates good music, good art, and good manners. My friend Bruno, twelve years old, has never been to school and is completely illiterate, but he is a perfect gentleman and a poet of life. Italian children are civilized.

3

The highest art of a civilized society is politics. The Italian political sense is developed to an almost unbelievable degree. I have tried for many years to make some sense out of the Italian political situation, particularly on the national level; I have not succeeded. Italian politics is too rarified, too subtle, too advanced for me. I am not ready for it; it is far more civilized than I am. I do know that an Italian politician hardly ever says what he means, but apparently other Italians know immediately what he means. I have learned that the obvious motivation is never the real motivation, and that, in Italy, the political realist seems cynical to an American.

Although the Italian constitution outlaws political strikes, almost all major strikes in Italy are patently political. Even when a strike is made in order to redress some grievance, the political dimension is always strong and usually primary. In fact, history's first recorded political strike was in the fifth century B.C. when the Roman people struck against the senate for an increase in civil rights.

Politics in Italy goes far beyond civil politics. There are ecclesiastical politics, business politics, school politics, family politics, and the politics of everyday living. The subtlest, and usually the most difficult for an American to understand, is Vatican politics. To begin with, Vatican politics is Italian; it is formulated and carried out by Italians, and can perhaps be understood only by Italians. It is a Catholic politics, in the service of God and the Church. Although sometimes misinformed and bungling, it has the wisdom of a serpent—if not always the simplicity of a dove. It is realistic, it has no illusions about human nature and motives. It is basically a politics not of justice but of compassion. It is Italian politics at its most Italian.

The average Italian, then, is a polished politician. His somewhat cynical approach to reality is tempered by his knowledge that something can always be worked out, some arrangement can be made, something will turn up, there will be a compromise in the end that will please everyone somewhat although perhaps no one completely. I explained to an Italian friend that Americans work at politics and at every kind of social relationship, that we are prepared when we move into a social or a political situation, that we do our homework. He replied, "We Italians are not always so well prepared, but we manage." The Italian manages. He can work something out. This is why Italians are so easy to deal with, why they are so reasonable. They adjust, they compromise, they give a little and they take a little. That is to say, they are civilized.

Civilization is largely a matter of style. It is a question of how one lives, reacts, interacts with others. Civilization is a matter of how things are done, a matter of doing with style. In Italy, style is everything. The emphasis is on the manner. In sculpture, painting and architecture, that modality which most stresses style, manner, effect, impression, is the baroque. Italian culture is, as it has been since the early seventeenth century, markedly baroque.

The term *baroque* is used mainly to denote a certain type of art and architecture that followed the Renaissance period in Europe; in the Catholic countries, the baroque style emerged from the more austere and mannered counter-Reformation style, and it dominated Italian art and architecture from the early seventeenth century into the eighteenth. In a more general sense, *baroque* designates a whole culture, European culture between the Renaissance and the Enlightenment. It is the last European culture organized on explicitly Christian principles. In the broadest sense, the word *baroque* can be applied to a certain spirit, to the spirit that lay behind baroque art and culture. Italian culture found itself in the baroque; it has been baroque in spirit for at least three centuries.

Just as in baroque architecture the façade is the all-important part of a building's exterior, so, too, in Italian life, putting up a front is all-important. To some this might suggest a certain falsity or intent to deceive, or at least a superficiality. Not for the Italian. It is important to dress well, to look good, to appear at one's best. Perhaps the best-dressed children in the world are the Italian children; they are also probably the best behaved and the most polite, but they do not seem at all suppressed or strained. The stress is not so much on correctness, as on flair, not on what is proper but on what is dazzling or at least pleasing. This is not superficiality; it is style.

It is Italian style. And it forms an important part of what meets the eye in Italian civilization.

9

From Split to Medjugorje: "My Peace I Give You"

The Blessed Virgin Mary has been appearing daily since June 1981 to a small group of young people in the parish church of Medjugorje, a village in the rocky hills of eastern Yugoslavia. Her message is: conversion, prayer and fasting, and—especially—peace. Through the young people to whom she comes and speaks for a few minutes every evening, she has asked that we call her "Our Lady of Peace." Early this year, I made plans to go there for a week to pray. Here is a short account of my trip.

1

Jugoslavian Airlines flight 401 takes me from Rome to Split, a city of 150,000 people on the Adriatic coast of the republic of Croatia, one of the five semi-autonomous political and ethnic regions that make up the nation of Yugoslavia. I arrive in the evening; I must spend the night in a hotel, since the next bus for Medjugorje leaves at eight o'clock the next morning.

I find my hotel in the main square of the medieval "old city," a large block of light-colored stone pavement, tightly packed buildings, and narrow arched streetways—all beautifully preserved. I feel I am walking on and in history. No cars or buses; I could be in the fifteenth century.

Outside the old city, down by the bus and train stations near the waterfront, many people, especially young men, walk aimlessly or mill around. I count five groups of young men singing—two in bars, three in the street. The songs all sound the same: completely tuneless, with a medium-slow rhythm, mechanically sung.

The people on this Sunday night give me the impression of lacking élan, hope, purpose. Pleasant up to a point, courteous for the most part, they expect nothing, and they give nothing. Simple people, but outside the standard Mediterranean stereotype; they are quite unlike, say, the Italians or the Spaniards or the Greeks. They lack any Mediterranean flair. They dress not so much poorly as badly; they do not have a certain suavity, what we used to call "cool." The women's hair looks awful; one wonders where Croatian hairdressers are trained. Even the mannequins in the store windows dress in poor taste and are ugly, nearly grotesque. Croatian charm does not lie in appearances. Rather in this: that they try hard to please, with a carefree incompetence. They are likeable.

Split, then, is a dull city, neither peaceful nor frenetic—just restless, aimless, colorless. Like the songs sung this evening, Split is tuneless, with a medium-slow pace that does not go anywhere definite. Split's medieval past is now and forever. Nothing changes. No future, and so no hope. It is a quiet city. But not a peaceful one.

Less than twenty percent of the Split population are practicing Catholics. Outside the cities, in the country, regular religious practice can go as high as ninety-five percent. But here in Split, communism has succeeded in reducing the importance and the practice of Catholicism. My destination, the village parish of Medjugorje, will be different.

2

I've been to Medjugorje three times before this. The first time, in the fall of 1981, I had heard of the apparitions of Our Lady, and I went by train from Rome to Split. There, I went to the archbishop's residence. Archbishop Frane Franic, a well-known theologian and an important figure of the Second Vatican Council, received me graciously, and sent me to Medjugorje in his car with a priest driver.

My second visit to Medjugorje resulted in a book, with Lucy Rooney, S.N.D., *Our Lady Queen of Peace: Medjugorje* (New York, Dublin, London, 1984). The third time, I went just to pray there for a few days. And I smuggled out a manuscript by Svetozar Kraljevic, later published as *The Apparitions of Our Lady at Medjugorje* (Chicago, 1984).

This time I carry no religious books or manuscripts either into or out of Yugoslavia. A Texan friend had previously tried to take Father Kraljevic's book manuscript to the U.S., was arrested by local police, and spent two awful days in a rural jail in Herzegovina. December 29, 1984, Father René Laurentin, the distinguished French theologian and expert on Marian apparitions, carried a few religious books on his way to Medjugorje; he was arrested, stripped naked, insulted, tried before a judge, fined heavily, given twelve hours to get out of the country, and forbidden to re-enter for a year.

Since I look neither prosperous nor important, the police never stop me. But I am careful just the same. Although a priest, I am wearing a necktie instead of a Roman collar, and I travel light. My confidence in my disguise is shattered, however, when the ticket-collector on the morning bus out of Split smiles at me and asks, "Medjugorje?" I admit it.

After a long ride along the Adriatic, and then inland along narrow winding roads through the rocks and brush of the harsh hills of Croatia and Herzegovia, at ten minutes to twelve, I see Saint James' Church, the parish church of Medjugorje, far off on my right. Five minutes later, the ticket-collector motions me to get off the bus. I do, and follow a sign that reads, "Medjugorje." A twenty-minute walk brings me to the church.

Walking, I notice all the new homes that have been built and that are being built. Some of these, and some of the older houses, have signs now: "*sobe, zimmer,* rooms, *chambre.*" The government, then, has granted a lot of building permits, and permission to take boarders. But, when I come to the church area, I see that the local communists have not relented in harassing the Franciscan sisters and priests. The sisters' convent burned down some years ago, but the local authorities will not grant any building permit for a new one. So four sisters and four priests have to share a small rectory built for one or two priests.

I have not telephoned ahead to tell the Franciscans of my arrival. Although other telephones in the area work quite well, the authorities have seen to it that the parish house telephone rarely functions. Telephoning from other countries is sometimes impossible; the calls are often blocked, sometimes by a pleasant chime. The Franciscans are surprised but happy to see me. And I am delighted to see them.

At five in the afternoon, we go to the church for the rosary. The church is already filling up. Hundreds of people join in saying the joyful and the sorrowful mysteries. We finish just before six, when the Mass begins. Tonight, Father Joseph Zovko is the principal celebrant. Father Zovko was the parish priest when the apparitions first began. The Yugoslavian government tried him for sedition and sentenced him to two and one half years at hard labor. After a year and a half of abuse, with no bible and breviary, forbidden to say Mass, he was freed. Vatican pressure obtained his release on condition that he would never again be assigned to Medjugorje. The local people say he went to prison because he refused to lock the young people out of his church in the evenings; evenings are when the apparitions take place.

In fact, Mary appears and speaks to two young men and two young women every night at about 5:45 in the church balcony. They wait for her there, reciting the rosary, sometimes alone and sometimes with one of the Franciscans. Promptly at 5:45 they kneel and begin to pray aloud, saying *Our Father's*, *Hail Mary's* and *Glory Be's* until, after they've prayed a short while, Our Lady appears. They say she looks like a young Croatian woman of that region: blue eyes, black hair, pink cheeks. She wears a long silver robe and a white veil; she stands, suspended in air, on a small grey cloud. They can see, hear, and touch her. The apparitions last only a few minutes.

Father Zovko preaches quite a long homily. No one stirs. Almost everyone goes to Holy Communion. After Mass, one of the parish priests prays over the people for healing, standing at the altar with arms extended, and praying aloud at some length. Then we say together the glorious mysteries of the rosary and the litany of Our Lady. The whole program takes three hours. Most of the people in the parish and many from the surrounding region do this every day.

3

What is it like at Medjugorje? Peaceful. Peaceful, even though under severe attack. The local bishop, highly emotional and impulsive, strongly opposes the five young people, the Franciscan priests and sisters, and the authenticity of the apparitions. Joining him is the whole Yugoslavian communist government structure, and especially the local country police force.

Many theologians, including Hans Urs von Balthasar, René Laurentin and Michael O'Carroll, have spoken out in favor of the truth of the events at Medjugorje. So has Archbishop Frane Franic of Split and many other churchmen. The Pope is said to be quite favorable to Medjugorje. But they are not there. The local bishop and the communist police are.

And yet, around the church and up on the hill where Mary first appeared, peace is in the air. I can feel it. It seeps in through the many layers of clothing I wear against the bitter cold, seeps into my heart. I learn at Medjugorje that peace is a gift, not earned or won or even built, but given as God's grace.

Peace comes to us from God through Mary, the mediatrix of all grace. It comes into our hearts as his gift. It comes to me here, at Medjugorje, now.

Peace, then, is not merely the absence of violence, nor is it simply good order and no disturbances. Peace is a positive quality. First of the heart, and then—when many hearts have it—of society. It is a grace, given in response to prayer and fasting to those who turn to God in conversion.

Peace cannot exist without hope, and—especially—without hope in some kind of ultimate destiny. Thus, peace cannot exist without religion.

When religious belief is missing, then our deepest aspirations—for God—are blocked, and we are inevitably restless. When our hearts are led to reach out to God, then there is partial fulfillment now of those longings, and the hope of ultimate fulfillment. And there comes peace. "You have made us for yourself, O Lord, and our hearts shall find no rest until they rest in you."

Mary, Mother of God,
my mother, Queen of Peace,
ask your Son Jesus
to give me the gift of peace.
Pray for me for peace:
peace in my heart,
peace of mind and of soul,
peace in my family,
peace with all whom I meet,
the peace of Jesus.

Jesus, my Lord and Savior,
my Brother, King of Peace,
I come to you with Mary, Queen of Peace,
to ask you humbly for a new outpouring
of the gift of peace.
Pour out on me your Holy Spirit of Peace.
Give me peace, Jesus,
peace within myself,
peace in my family,
peace in my everyday life.

Give peace to my nation, and to all nations,
peace among all peoples,
peace in the world.

Jesus, my mediator with the Father
take me to the Father to pray for peace.

Father, Father of Jesus,
our Father, my Father,
I come to you with your Son Jesus.
In him and with him and through him
I pray for peace:
peace inside me,
peace around me,
peace in the world.
Amen.

10

South of Naples:
A Call to Prayer

1

South of Naples, about one and one half hour's drive going still further south from Salerno on the motorway and then, from the city of Eboli, moving inland on the regional road that winds through the hills, you can see Oliveto Citra (population about 3500) well before you get there. It sits on one end of a loaf-like hill, built for defense, the houses piled together in a heap and topped by the castle. Up close, you can see that much of the town was destroyed in the 1980 earthquake. Many families continue to live in temporary prefabricated dwellings.

The main industry here is farming. In most Italian communities the farmers live in towns, but here they live near the land. This explains the numerous white red-roofed houses dotting the valley of the Sele River below the town.

Oliveto Citra has one Catholic parish, one priest, Monsignor Giuseppe Amato, and until recently few practicing Catholics. In the last municipal elections, May 1985, the town voted almost unanimously for the Communist mayor and a Communist town council.

The narrow streets of the town can hold only one car; they do not permit two-way traffic. The main street that runs through the town has a traffic light at each end to regulate the automobiles so that traffic can flow in only one direction at a time.

The main street passes through the central square, Piazza Garibaldi, and then through a small unnamed square. To the right, just beyond the little square, you can see the baroque facade of the parish church, Our Lady of Mercy. The church, badly damaged during the 1980 earthquake, remains closed until the government can repair it. Monsignor Amato says Mass in a small prefabricated shelter still further down the road on a flat plain with the prefabricated temporary houses of those whom the 1980 earthquake displaced.

Across from the old church, on higher ground, looms the castle. Built in 1145, used during World War II and after for drying animal skins, its ruins further destroyed by the 1980 earthquake, the castle stands locked up, closed to visitors. An old stone stairway leads from the little square up to a fence and gate made of vertical iron bars. A rusty chain and padlock hold the gate closed.

Inside the gate the branches of bushes hold rosaries of various colors. The bushes look like exotic plants with rosaries for fruit. Flowers line the walkway up from the gate along the wall of the castle.

This is where Our Lady is said to come every evening since May 1985.

2

Saint Macarius, the patron saint of Oliveto Citra, has his feast-day on May 24th. About ten o'clock in the evening on the feast of Saint Macarius, 1985, twelve small boys played in the little square just off Piazza Garibaldi. The townspeople had gathered in Piazza Garibaldi to celebrate the feast, which in Oliveto Citra takes the form of a civil rather than a religious observance. The music and singing filtered through the narrow passage between buildings where the main street connects the larger square to the small one where the boys played.

Suddenly the boys heard a baby crying. The baby's voice came from the other side of the old iron castle gate. Several of the boys, alarmed, frightened, excited, ran back and forth between the little square and Piazza Garibaldi. Finally one boy threw a stone at the gate. The stone went inside the castle grounds, but seemed to strike nothing and not to fall to the ground. Frightened, the boys ran, then returned.

And, almost immediately, a woman appeared. Or something. Different boys saw different things.

A few saw a light or a luminous shape, or a light shaped like a person. Several saw a young woman. Some saw an infant in her arms. Others did not. But they each saw something.

The twelve boys, all about ten or twelve years old, ran into the Iannece Bar in the Piazza Garibaldi shouting, "We've seen the Blessed Virgin Mary." Silvia Iannece, twenty-five years old, born and raised in Peterborough, England, behind the bar, believed them. Her assistant, Anita Rio, said, "Come on! How could these boys have seen the Blessed Virgin Mary?" The boys said, "It's true; come and see." And they ran back to the little square with the gate to the castle.

Anita Rio, curious, followed behind them. When she caught up with them at the castle gate, she saw, beyond the gate, a young woman of indescribable beauty dressed in a white robe and wearing a blue mantle with a filigreed gold border. A crown of stars encircled her head. She carried an infant in her right arm. The infant held a rosary in his hands.

Anita, frightened, backed up. The young woman motioned to her with her free hand, beckoning her to come forward. The woman said to Anita, "You will see me at night."

Anita was taken to the hospital in a state of shock. The doctor on duty, Giuseppe Santelli, when told the apparent reason for her condition, asked her several questions to ascertain her general psychological state. His diagnosis: "This girl is healthy in body and in mind; she has an obvious muscular tension as though something has caused her great fear."

Early in 1986 I went to Oliveto Citra. I spoke with some of the boys who had played in the small square and who had seen something on May 24th, with Anita Rio, and with others including the parish priest. In the evening I went to the castle gate in the little square to say the rosary, to sing hymns, to pray.

3

A cold wind blows through the little square on this particular Monday evening when I come to pray at the gate of the castle. I have come fairly late. Already, about 5:30 this evening, a large group has met to say all fifteen mysteries of the rosary, to sing hymns, and to pray in the square and at the top of the steps at the castle gate.

Tonight is quiet. Last night, Sunday, more than twenty bus-loads of pilgrims came. And the "Evangelicals" came, members of an American-financed Pentecostal church here in Oliveto Citra. They come from time to time to heckle. Many of them members of the Christian Democratic party and all of them believing Christians, they love Jesus but they hate what's going on at the castle gate. When they come, they stand apart, shout abuse, and try to drown out the Catholic singing with their own hymns. But tonight, they stayed home.

At 8:30 the rosary begins. We go right through all fifteen mysteries, led by people speaking through a microphone hooked up to amplifiers in the square. We pray in a group of about one hundred and eighty people. Our backs to the buildings behind us, we face the gate to the castle and the stone stairs leading up to it. The ruins of the ancient Norman castle stand over us on the right. Piazza Garibaldi is on our left. An occasional automobile following the main street through town passes between us and the stairway to the castle gate.

After the rosary we say the litany of Our Lady. It all takes about an hour and ten minutes.

People go to the gate to pray for a few minutes after the rosary and the litany. But only eight or ten people at a time can go to the gate, because the gate is only about ten feet wide. I go in the first shift of ten people. I do pray at the gate. But I also look around to see what the others are doing. I notice one man in particular, in work clothes, who seems immobilized as though in an ecstasy. I will meet him later back down in the square. He sees Our Lady regularly.

A young man named Pinuccio regulates the traffic. After my shift has prayed at the gate for four or five minutes, Pinuccio calls us to return into the square, and he moves the next shift of ten people up to the gate.

In the meantime, while a few people pray at the castle gate, the others sing hymns, pray, and have a kind of prayer meeting. Monsignor Giuseppe Amato, the parish pastor, known locally and with great affection as Don Peppino, gives a short talk. He says that pilgrims should not be disappointed if they do not see Our Lady; she is here with us, present to us.

I know most of the hymns that we sing. But one hymn, quite long, I have never heard before. It is called, "Queen of the Castle," and it is a hymn to Our Lady. Here is the story behind the hymn.

In the autumn of 1985 Albino Coglianese, the head of the parish committee that leads the evening prayer and collects written testimonies, wrote the words to "Queen of the Castle" so that they could be sung to an old southern Italian folk melody. The hymn has seven fairly long verses.

On Tuesday evening, October 29th, 1985, at 8:45, Mafalda Caputo took the microphone in the little piazza in order to lead the rosary. Before she could begin, she saw a luminous shape and heard Our Lady's voice inviting her to sing the hymn, and began to lead the singing. She started the first verse singing the folk melody, according to the way that the hymn had been sung up to that moment.

She heard Our Lady say, "Don't sing it that way; listen to the choir and learn the melody and teach it to the others." Mafalda did not see any choir, but she heard the hymn sung by beautiful voices, at first distant and then coming closer. She listened and learned the melody and taught it to those present.

Not only Mafalda heard the heavenly choir. In the parish office are documents signed by several persons of various ages stating that they too heard the invisible choir sing Albino Coglianese's hymn, "Queen of the Castle," to a new melody. Several weeks later, Our Lady told Mafalda that the melody sung by the choir in heaven is an ancient and long-forgotten melody of the region around Oliveto Citra.

"Queen of the Castle" has become the song of those who come to the castle gate in the little square. They sing it, now of course with the melody taught by the heavenly choir, every night.

The praying and hymn-singing end at about ten o'clock. Some people leave, but most stay in the little square to talk or to pray by themselves. Some go up to the castle gate to pray.

At ten-thirty, as it does every evening at this time, the parish committee for the apparitions meets to evaluate how the evening went. One by one, they go up the stairway of number twelve in the little square, directly opposite the castle gate, to the committee office.

The committee has ten members: eight men of the parish; the pastor, Don Peppino; and Anna De Bellis, the mother of two small children who see Our Lady frequently. Albino Coglianese, who wrote the words for the hymn, "Queen of the Castle," co-ordinates the committee.

Albino is a heavy-set middle-aged man with a full grey beard. He moves slowly and speaks deliberately. He works as a surveyor and building consultant, and was chairman of the local Socialist party for seven years. Recently he formed a small group of "Christians for Socialism."

There are a number of things to discuss this evening. Four pilgrims have turned in written witnesses saying that they saw Our Lady tonight at the castle gate; these need to be evaluated and turned over to the parish priest, Don Peppino. And there are several items held over from previous meetings.

A man enters the office to make a financial contribution. A committee member tells him that his money will go toward the building of a small chapel near the castle gate, and gives him a receipt. Every contribution here is recorded, and every donor is given a receipt.

Before the committee meeting begins, I leave to go back down into the little square.

Several people still stand around. Some pray at the gate. I turn left down the short connecting street to Piazza Garibaldi and go into the Iannece bar. Michael Iannece, the proprietor, won't let me pay for my coffee.

I walk back to the castle gate. It is now about 11:15. Several people still pray at the gate.

4

In the parish at Oliveto Citra, Don Peppino says, there are about twenty persons to whom Our Lady has appeared several times. Albino Coglianese, the head of the parish committee for the apparitions, says that there is as yet no fixed group of "visionaries"; it has not settled yet. Perhaps some who have seen Our Lady several times may stop seeing her, or have already stopped. Others may go on seeing her for some time. Maybe, eventually, there will be fixed group of people at Oliveto Citra whom Our Lady visits with a certain frequency.

There is, however, no group like the children at Fatima or like the small group at Medjugorje in Yugoslavia. There seems to be no particular unity among the people Our Lady has chosen at Olivetto Citra. The only common point of reference is Our Lady herself.

Besides some of the boys who first saw Mary, and Anita Rio, I met and spoke with a number of other persons who see Our Lady frequently: two children, an automobile mechanic, a thirteen-year-old girl from a nearby town, a housewife and mother, a sixteen-year-old boy who works as a carpenter, a construction worker with a large family, four of the original twelve boys who saw Our Lady in May, 1985, and Anita Rio.

Oliveto Citra lies in the diocese of Campagna. Several years ago the Campagna diocese was put directly under the head of the Archdiocese of Salerno, Archbishop Guerino Grimaldi, who is therefore also the Bishop of Campagna. For ordinary administration, however, the diocese of Campagna has its own vicar general, Monsignor Giuseppe Amato, the pastor of the parish of Oliveto Citra, Don Peppino.

The events at Oliveto Citra in many ways center on Don Peppino. The persons who see Our Lady frequently have little contact with one another. They have, in fact, almost nothing in common except their extraordinary contacts with Our Lady. But they all refer what they see and hear to Don Peppino. He keeps the records, the signed testimonies, and any other documents. He is, to one degree or another, their spiritual director. They all love him and trust him.

Don Peppino is not just an ordinary parish priest. As vicar of a diocese, he carries many of the responsibilities of a bishop. He is slow to speak and to act, wise, prudent, and warmly affable. He radiates common sense, good judgement, dependability and strength of character. He loves his people and takes responsibility for pastoring them.

What does he think about the apparitions? At first quite sceptical, Don Peppino soon took into account the spiritual fruits of what was happening—the conversions, the increased attendance at Sunday Mass, the whole new spirit in his parish. He knows that the same credibility cannot be given to everything that goes on in his parish. Not everyone who says, "I have seen Our Lady" has necessarily really seen her.

But it is quite clear to the pastor that Our Lady has come to Oliveto Citra in a new and extraordinary way, that she has made herself seen and heard in his parish and especially at the gate of the castle many times and to many different people. And that what Our Lady says and does in his parish has meaning for the world outside Oliveto Citra, for the whole Church, and for all mankind.

What he finds special about the apparitions here is that, in the past, in other parts of the world, Our Lady has appeared several times to one or to a few people. But here, he says, she has already appeared hundreds, even thousands of times to hundreds of people. This has never happened before in the history of Marian apparitions.

Our Lady, and Don Peppino underlines the fact, calls us to prayer. She calls us urgently and sincerely. She is displeased when the rosary is said poorly. She wants us to pray the rosary, and to pray it fervently, prayerfully.

She calls us to pray for the world, for sinners, for peace. She calls the people here to pray not only for the people of Oliveto Citra, because they need conversion so badly, but for all mankind.

11

Pelicans in Florida

1

All the birds. Terns, gulls, egrets, ducks, herons. And the pelicans. At dusk, a pelican settles on each of the poles in two parallel rows in the water, extending out from shore like the pier they used to support. One pelican for each pole. I see them in the morning, still asleep at dawn.

At the time of Jesus, pelicans lived on the Sea of Galilee. Maybe they slept on poles there as they do here in this quiet backwater of Tampa Bay, Florida. At night, I can see Saint Petersburg twenty miles across the bay. I can see the lights of Tampa off to the left. And the cars moving along Highway Sixty that lines the bay. And the pelicans.

In Christian symbolism, the pelican stands for Jesus. In particular, the pelican stands for the tender care that Jesus has for each of us.

The pelican's long beak contains a sack that holds small fish with which it nourishes its children. The pelican gets the food out of its bill by pressing the sack against its neck; the food ejects into the mouths of the baby pelicans. It seems that the adult pelican is opening its chest with its beak, an illusion augmented by the reddish cast of its breast.

From the second century on, Christianity has interpreted the pelican as a symbol of Jesus Christ who has saved us by his death on the cross, where his side was pierced with a lance, and water and blood came out. By death, Jesus has nourished us into salvation, has redeemed us to eternal life.

By the late middle ages, the pelican had become a symbol not only of the redeeming Christ, but also of the Eucharist in which Jesus feeds us with his own body and blood. In the baroque churches of my neighborhood in the center of Rome, you can find the pelican ornamenting altars, chalices, and tabernacle doors.

I feel the tender and nurturing care of Jesus here in the peace of Tampa Bay. I have a quiet retreat house to myself for a few days before Christmas. To pray and to rest. Along with the pelicans, and with the Lord. I find myself simply enjoying the Lord's personal love and the peace of this place, his peace and his place.

2

Christmas day, early, I pack Mass equipment and vestments into a Toyota generously lent to me, and drive on calm dark highways north to my brother's. I find the same peace here, in his house, Christmas peace, Christ's peace with us. I find his peace in my sister-in-law's loving and tender care that takes the form of a scrambled eggs and grits breakfast. I find it in my brother playing with his grandson, nourishing him on grandfatherly love and unspoken wisdom. I find the peace of Jesus in the tender and nurturing love that everyone has for everyone else.

We have Mass before Christmas dinner, standing around the dining-room table. Jesus nourishes us with his body and his blood. And I see his peace in my brother's profound and reverent prayerfulness, in my sister-in-law's obvious love for us and for God, and in the humility and baffled incomprehension of my niece's Protestant husband who stands with us at, in, the Mass, unconsciously radiating goodness and sharing somehow in the food Christ gives us.

Grant us, Lord, the peace that flows in rays from your pierced and now risen and glorified heart. Help us to love, to love you more, to love those you have put us with in this life. And, loving, to give your peace to others. Bring us all to the life to come, eternal peace, to share it in love together, together with you. Amen.

12

Reflection

After having written these chapters at various times in their respective localities, I look back and find to my surprise that what has stayed with me most are not the images in those chapters but rather certain other, seemingly banal and uninteresting picture-memories. The way the girl in the Bucharest hotel lobby obviously felt flattered that I paid attention to her and valued her ideas. The mother and her two small children, a boy and a tiny girl, that I saw one morning from my terrace through a skylight in a close by and lower building in the center of Jerusalem. The mother moved about the kitchen making breakfast for her children, then watched them eat it, and sent them with their books off to school.

Nigerians riding the bus with me from Jos to Kano, sitting ahead of me, the backs of their heads increasingly familiar with the journey's bumpy progress. The other priests and I vesting in the sacristy before Mass at the Derry Charismatic Conference. Three women in Harare, one black, one white, one of mixed race, close friends, coming together to church, getting out of the car talking and laughing.

I did not include these memory pictures nor others like them because they could have come from any culture, from any part of the world. They represent not differences but likenesses, the likeness of the humanity we hold in common. They stay in my mind and come to the front of my imagination so easily precisely because of that. What we have in common has a far greater importance than our differences.